I thought you should get into the mood of the country

love

Anne
X

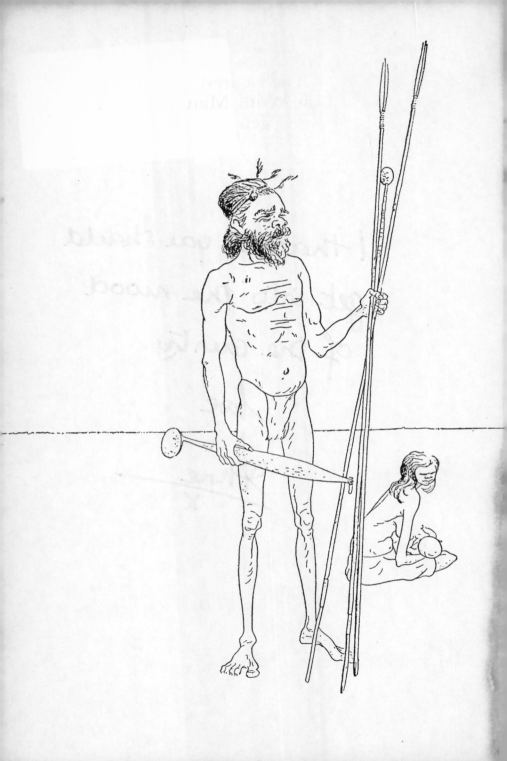

The Nearest the White Man gets

Aboriginal Narratives
and Poems of New South Wales
collected by

ROLAND ROBINSON

with an introductory essay by
Norman Talbot

Hale & Iremonger

Drawings of The Aboriginal People
Roderick Shaw

Typeset, printed & bound by
Southwood Press Pty Limited
80–92 Chapel Street, Marrickville, NSW

For *the publisher*
Hale & Iremonger Pty Limited
GPO Box 2552, Sydney, NSW

National Library of Australia Cataloguing-in-publication entry

Roland Robinson, 1912-
    The Nearest the White Man gets.

    ISBN 0 86806 379 7 (paperbound)

    1. Aborigines, Australian — New South Wales
    — Legends. 2. Aborigines, Australian — New
    South Wales — Poetry.

398.2'09944

Publication assisted by the Literature Board of the
Australia Council, the Federal Government's arts
funding and advisory body.

To Jacqueline Diplock

Contents

Aboriginal people, from wartime drawings by Roderick Shaw, are inserted not as illustrations to text, but as a general introduction to the Aborigines.
The Aboriginal drawings are from Roland Robinson's *Feathered Serpent*, published in 1956.
The cover and general design are by Roderick Shaw.

Introduction

In 1986 I was invited to compile the New South Wales poetry anthology *Another Site to be Mined* (*Poetry Australia*, Double Issue 107/108), and of that very assorted collection the work that brought most comment and enthusiasm was Roland Robinson's setting down of Thomas Kelly's beautiful narration 'Geerdung the Maker'. Some regarded it as prose, others as a 'prose poem', but all remarked on its unforgettable and evocative simplicity.

Simplicity does not mean naivety. The world of this story has been submerged by a more visible but possibly less resilient Australia. Our assumption that we have subdued nature is also seen as skin deep, as the family crouches helpless under the menace of the cyclonic storm. Responding to the calm completeness of faith in 'the old lady, the princess', we may also feel that our assumptions about Aboriginal religion are totally inadequate, based as they are on the necessarily dismissive comments of Christian pastors and converts.

Thomas Kelly evokes not only the many years of White Australian dominance over the lives and the traditions of Aboriginal people, but also the integrity and persistence of those traditions. Yes, even in places where we have no right to expect it, in a shabby, inconspicuous man hitching out of Sydney to go 'back up north', stories like this are alive. How dare we assume that the only 'real Aboriginals' are tiny tribal groups of full-bloods, following their endless walkabout through the semi-deserts of the far inland? The seductions of our civilisation have not been quite that irresistible!

The setting out of these stories may seem arbitrary, but is dictated by the sense of place essential to most Aboriginal narrative. The first section is from the South Coast of New South Wales, and begins with a genuinely mythical sea-coast story which Roland says was 'the first story which led me to realise that such myths, the oral part of tribal rituals, still exist among "dark people" near the main cities'.

Of the many stories about clever-fellas, those whose luck, talent and self-confidence, whether or not linked to deep spiritual knowledge, makes them outstanding, two Wallaga Lake stories employ the idea of a stone as a totem. 'Adam Cooper' is a fine, casual example of the whole man in Aboriginal terms, but the vulnerability of mortals to their own sources of power and protection is more brilliantly conveyed by 'Rites of Passage'.

'Billy Bamboo' is autobiographical, and obviously cut to fit Roland's cloth: 'You're a bit of a blackfeller, you try it.' Old Billy, almost blind and more or less confined to the Mission at Wallaga Lake, seems incredibly calm about the massacre of his father's tribe by white riflemen, placing it beside the tribal war that left his mother to be reared by whites. In all the stories of Percy Mumbulla which follow, that same equanimity, that sense that what is done is unchangeable, can be found.

Percy Mumbulla is quintessentially a 'natural' storyteller, and the free-flowing prose-poem form of Roland's presentation is exactly appropriate to most of his stories, giving a certain formality to the line-endings without the elaborate fuss of superadded rhyme. However, the following poem which Roland crafted from Percy's description of the place of milk and honey, Abraham's Bosom, has been frequently reprinted, and in any case, Roland comments, 'Percy gave it his O.K.' Here it may serve to show the savour that the poet re-creates from the story, for once blending perfectly with the formal restraint of couplets and the conscious shapeliness of the last line's vocal and temporal 'frame'.

Bees

Abraham's Bosom was the name
the place had after the white man came.
From the holler trees in their home
them old fellers cut the honey-comb.
On honey an' little white grubs they fed,
'cause them young bees were blackfellers' bread.
That's why they was so mighty an' strong
in their native home at Currarong.
An' them old fellers' drink was honey-bul,
honey an' water, a coolamon full.
Naked through the bush they went,
an' never knew what sickness meant.
Them little dark bees could do you no harm,
they'd crawl all over your honey-smeared arm.
But them Eyetalian bees, they'd bung
your eyes right up. When we was young,

we used to rob their honey trees.
Savage! They'd fetch your blood. Them bees
would zing an' zoom, an' chase a feller
from Bomaderry to Bodalla.
Well, old Uncle Minah, old Billy Bulloo,
Jacky Mumbulla, King Merriman too,
them fierce old fellers, they're all gone now.
An' the wild honey's still in the gum tree bough.

Percy Mumbulla's stories are not, like Fred Biggs', myths. Rather, they are a response of unwearied, attentive interest in the interwoven lives of his people, the bush and the sea around them, and the encroaching greed and trash of white Australia. If figures like 'Uncle Minah, old Billy Bulloo' reach legendary status, they do so without narrative fanfare, by their own natures, as it were. Even as a boy, Percy had followed the old men, the repositories of the male line of tribal wisdom, rather than younger, more confused heroes. Yet he is not a myth-carrier, as they were. This comes out in his stories of the behaviour of animals, brilliantly and amusingly observed, but as far from the talking-animal stories of Maria Boney as they are from Aesop's didactic fables.

Maria Boney, from Brewarrina, tells of animals behaving like people. In the golden age, clearly, all living things were people and akin to the Aboriginals. These metamorphosis stories assume the kinship of all the inhabitants of the land; they imply, energise and adorn central aspects of our relationship to our environment, aspects which white environmentalists are only now ready to welcome.

Fred Biggs, from Lake Carjelligo, is not only closer to mythic time than most of the coastal story-tellers, he is also capable of the sublime cadences of the poet appropriate to mythic matters. 'Mapooram' is one of Australia's great poems, and the other three collected here, though less widely loved, are of at least comparable stature.

The remainder of the collection comes from the North Coast, much of it from the little settlement of Woodenbong. The poems are loosely grouped with animal descriptions first, and material with strong religious elements last. Of course, none of this final group are, in this form, 'butherum', or sacred stories, though they are certainly related to them.

Among fascinating comparisons this book affords is the porpoise-killer story, which can be set beside Percy Mumbulla's south coast whaling memory, and the two versions of the battle where Arracoon Racecourse is. Of particular interest is the double creator-journey, the first by the divine being Nguthungulli and the second by the culture-hero Wao, beside which I have set the poem that Roland has derived from the story. His own pursuit of the tales of Dirrangun up the Clarence River makes him a worthy successor; how shrewdly did the Aboriginals of Woodenbong name him Wao!

In his autobiographical volumes, *The Drift of Things* (1973) and *The Shift of Sands* (1976), Roland tells much of his relationships with various Aboriginal peoples and their traditions. The tales he collected from Northern and Central Australia are autonomous, but the destructive and inescapable changes that frazzle the edges of the New South Wales tradition can make the resultant stories intensely moving. Even Fred Biggs, still within New South Wales, would hardly have felt tempted to include a reference to the Christian virgin birth story in his 'The Child who had no Father', but the coastal exposure to white Australia has been unremitting.

Here is an example of an unadulterated creation-myth that Roland collected from the story-teller Manoowa at Milingimbi, in far North Australia. His search for the stories that express not only Aboriginal but pan-human aspects of the human psyche is precisely rewarded by stories such as this.

The Two Sisters

On the Island of the Spirits of the Dead,
one of two sisters talks.
'We must make a canoe and follow the way
the sun walks.'

They've filled the canoe with sacred
rannga things,
and paddled away into the night
singing ritual songs.

'Sister, look back!' the first sister calls.
'Do you see the morning star?'
Her sister looks out along their wake.
'Nothing. Nothing's there.'

The little sister has fallen asleep.
Again her sister calls,
'Sister, look back for the morning star.'
'Nothing. Nothing at all.'

A spear of light is thrown across
the sea and lies far
ahead upon the sisters' course.
'Sister, the morning star.'

The sun comes up and walks the sky.
A fish with whiskers swims
ahead, and leaps out of the sea,
while the sisters sing.

Day and night, and day and night,
the sisters are gone
with the morning star and the leaping fish
and the sky-walking sun.

The sisters, hoar with dried salt spray,
the semen of the sea,
make landfall where parrots scream
from paperbark trees.

The sisters beach the bark canoe,
unload the rannga things.
They thrust one in the earth. From there
the first goanna comes.

They've gone inland. Their digging sticks
make sacred springs.
They leave behind them rannga forms
for all living things.

Out gathering food, the sisters have hung
their dilly-bags in a tree.
While they're away, men come and steal
their sacred ceremonies.

The sisters hear men singing and
song-sticks' 'Tjong-tjong'.
'Cover your ears. We cannot hear
the sacred song.'

'O, all our sacred ceremonies
belong now to the men.
We must gather food, and bear
and rear children.'

The relationship between our physical world and the 'Island of
the Spirits of the Dead' is not explained, nor is there any hint that it
needs to be explained. Perhaps it was north and west, across the
Arafura Sea. Such unforgettable details as the salt-crust, 'the
semen of the sea', are presented circumstantially, and although we
may recognise a kinship with the tradition of Aphrodite Ana-
dyomene here, or with a different story in the theme of the
guidance of the morning star, no European parallel can have been
deliberately invoked. Compare Alec Vesper or John Flanders, in
this book, with their intense awareness of the presence of the Bible.

Most striking in 'The Two Sisters' is the act of masculine theft
that ends the poem and makes the sisters' world resemble our own
with a painfully ironic directness. The episode is mythic in its logic:
the stories of Adam and Eve, Odin, Krishna, Zeus and many others
of our heroes involve an act of creative theft or betrayal. Here, the
dignity and restraint of the sisters' reaction speaks volumes about
the role of women in Aboriginal tribal society. It also strengthens
the unprovable suppositions about an ancient matriarchal stage in
tribal development posited in their different ways by anthropol-
ogists like Margaret Mead and intuitive writers like Robert
Graves, especially in *The White Goddess*.

Roland's choice of the ballad stanza is highly appropriate,
because this poem has the exalted status of 'rannga' itself: creative
and life-giving, inviting its audience to see their ancient ceremonies in a new and stimulating way, the story should be presented
in a form both energetic and recognisably traditional. As a creative
listener, rather than an anthropologist, he has had a wide range of
alternatives open to him. A verbatim record is appropriate for
some tales, and a re-working into English verse to translate the
spirit, rather than the letter, is his obvious duty for others.

Roland Robinson's life has been a complex love-affair with Australia, and this book is a collaboration between his turbulent and graceful personality and the Aboriginals of New South Wales, especially in those areas where the outward form of Aboriginal tradition might seem, to the white observer, to have been lost. The tellers of these hard, sweet, magical tales are not the revered elders of a visible tribe but the ordinary housewives, bean-pickers, timber-getters, railway workers, the easily ignored lowest stratum of our success-defined society. These are the voices of the hewers of wood and the drawers of water; we condescend to them at our spiritual peril!

How do such uneducated and insignificant people come to be such soul-stirring poets? In part this is because it was Roland Robinson who recorded their songs and stories; his incomparable ear and unselfconscious delight in what he heard may have brought out the best in the tale-tellers. More important still, though, is the sixty thousand or more years of non-literate culture, of delighted participation in sophisticated oral art, of attuning poet and audience one to the other. The pattern of poetry has come to be almost 'natural' — as it may have been to the Angles and Vikings of my ancestry. The ultimate word-processor is the human, communal mouth and ear. Why should an elderly woman not sit down on her earthen floor and sing for her odd but charismatic white visitor the songs of her childhood? She certainly wouldn't stop to think, 'But I'm no poet: I'd only spoil it.'

Almost all the artists who told these stories to Roland Robinson are now dead. That does not imply that such stories can no longer be found by people of good will. They are, though, unlikely to be told to the academically expert and detached cultural anthropologist with the state-of-the-art tape-recorder. The slightest sign of white condescension, or of a distancing technology apparently designed to steal the remnants of cultural identity from the blacks, is fatal. Young black collectors, especially if they are able to express their interest and enthusiasm with genuine warmth, have by far the best chance of making further collections.

And there is the key to this book. Roland Robinson's responses are passionate rather than analytic. His convictions about myth and legend are Jungian rather than post-Levi-Straussian. But poetry begets poetry: open fascination and grateful delight are the best possible tools for 'research' of this kind.

It will be obvious that certain Aboriginal words like *bugeen*, *wirreengun* in the southern part of the collection and *buloogan*, *wee-un*, *maragun*, *borrgorr* and *jurraveel* are not susceptible to precise translation. In each case the word has been retained in its Aboriginal form. Variations in pronunciation have been retained, since there is no clear evidence which pronunciation should be preferred. Thus, one northern tale presents *borrgorr* as *burraga*, another gives *birroogan* for *buloogan*. The sounds that Roland heard are the sounds he recorded.

In the same way, variant names given by individual northern story-tellers to their tribes or clans are retained, even when the probability is that they are actually referring to the same word, as with *gullibull*, *gilhavul*, *gindavul* and *githavul*.

These poems and stories, story-poems and poetic-prose anec-dotes, range from the wholly reshaped and versified material of 'The Song of Wao' to the verbatim record of the story-tellers' words in 'The Song of Darmunjura', where I can almost hear the un-pretentious energy of Dick Donnelly's voice, the common man as unhesitatingly exalted bard. In general, I am more moved by the latter than by the former, and I suspect, too, that Roland's later recordings are somewhat more successful in their own terms than the earlier ones.

Who is Roland Robinson? The answer would fill, already does fill, volumes. This passage from *The Shift of Sands* may be enough for our purposes here:

I am akin to the Aboriginals. For most of my life I have been a nomad, travelling the bushes of Australia like an Irish tinker, or like Clancy of the Overflow on my champion cattle drafter, Ovens. I've slept in caves, shacks, siding-sheds, shakedown shelters, fed, filled my hunger for hard ground. I've slept in the flowering coastal scrub with the stars over me. I've thrown my swag down all around, and over Australia. What is my Aborigi-nal name at Woodenbong? It is Wao, the name of the man who chased the two emus right across Australia and returned with the song of the God, Nguthungulli. (p. 281)

Certainly, Roland has eaten the honey of the muses, as described to him by James McGrath at the end of his story, 'The Brolgas':

The old people, they couldn't read or write, but they had their stories in their mouths and they had them in their hands. They danced and they sang all their stories.

You, you would be able to talk their language in an hour. They would get the native-honey and sing it and give it to you to eat. When you had eaten that honey you would be able to talk their language the same as they do.

Norman Talbot

New South Wales South Coast

Bundoola, the King of the Sea
Related by David Carpenter

One time we were cutting grass-trees near Spunder Hill. We had a stranger with us and my uncle told this stranger not to roll stones down the cliff. He told him that we'd have rain if he did. Well, this stranger went and rolled stones down. That night she teemed. It rained for a week, solid rain for a week. We lost two ton of grass-tree over it. We had it all cut and thrashed and bagged. It was the spirit of old Bundoola that made that rain. His spirit is there to this day. It'll never die out.

Bundoola was a native of the Kiola tribe. He lived at what they call Murramarang Mountain. He was a clever-feller. He was as good as a *bugeen*, and better.

Bundoola was the king of all fishermen. He supplied all his tribe with fish. Yes, mullet and groper and snapper. Only the best for Bundoola.

Bundoola could make the sea, the winds, the lightning and the rain do anything he wanted. He could make the sea rough or he could make it calm. He could make all kinds of different winds blow. When he wanted fish he would make the sea very rough and that westerly wind blow. He'd go out in this rough weather in his canoe and spear his fish. No matter if the sea was high, over the canoe. He could see the fish in the waves coming towards him. He would spear the fish in the waves.

He'd travel on this coast from north to south by canoe.

Bundoola's wife used to live on top of Smarts Mountain. Bundoola had two other women. These two other women were his fancy wives. You couldn't go and choose your wife in them days. Your wife was given to you in the rules of the tribe.

19

Bundoola had two little kiddies by his real wife. But he didn't like her. He liked his fancy wives. He'd give his real wife all the rotten fish, but the good fish he'd give to his other women.

Bundoola destroyed his wife. He turned her into stone. He was taking her away from Kiola and she looked back. He told her he'd destroy her. He turned the two little kiddies into stone. That was the rule of the *bugeen*. When they took a woman away and she looked back, they destroyed her.

The Kiola king sent a man to look for Bundoola. When they found that he had destroyed his wife, the king's orders were that Bundoola had to be destroyed.

They sent a man from north to south to look for a deep high gorge. They took Bundoola to Fitzroy Falls. You know how steep them Falls are. Well, they tied his arms and legs with wild vines. They tied him up in wild vines and lowered him over the Falls. They kept lowering him up and down, up and down from the ledge. That was his punishment for destroying his wife.

At last, as Bundoola was hanging over the falls, they cut the vine rope with a stone-axe. He dropped, but as soon as he hit the bottom he was gone. He was too clever.

Bundoola was gone for two days. They sent two *doowan*, men who fly through the air, after him. They picked him up at Point Perpendicular at Jervis Bay. The king's order was to destroy him there.

They took him to Spunder Hill, south of Currarong. They got him by water. They tied him with vines and lowered him over the cliff and into the sea. That was the only way they could destroy Bundoola.

Bundoola's bark canoe was turned into stone at Spunder Hill. You can only get to this place by boat. It's a sheer drop down from the cliff.

That canoe has fish in it, mullet and snapper and groper all tied up in vines and turned into stone. There in that canoe are the two knee-marks where Bundoola knelt.

Any stranger can go to Spunder Hill and roll stones down

the cliff and make it rain. He's making that spirit angry. You can take a stranger there in a boat and the sea will get as rough as billy-oh. The water will spout up from a big cunjevoi there about three feet round. That's him himself doing that. That's Bundoola's spirit.

He could wreck any canoe at sea. When he wanted to do this he had a fire-stick. He'd make a fire and pile on kelp. When the kelp burned it would crack like a gun going off. That was how he made rough weather to stop any stranger going there.

Make no mistake, that ole bloke's spirit is still there. It'll never die out.

22

Billy Bamboo
Related by Billy Bamboo, Wallaga Lake

This wild cherry tree makes a good shade.
I lie down under it and go to sleep.
By and by I hear a roaring sound.
'Oh, thunder storm coming up. I'll soon
fix him.' I break a branch off this tree
and burn it. The smoke goes straight up
into the sky. Those big rolling clouds
divide, one cloud goes one way, one cloud
the other way. You hear thunder rolling
down the sky.

This is our sacred tree.
It belongs to all the blackfellers. You're a bit
of a blackfeller, you try it. You'll say,
'That's true what old Billy Bamboo says.'

Well, my tribe got shot up. A white man found
a baby near the camp and took it back
to the station on his horse. That baby grew up
to be my father.

A Victorian tribe fought
the Wallaga Lake tribe. An old man and his wife
were running away along a path, carrying
a baby with them. They saw a big log hollowed out
by fire. They put the baby inside the log
and ran on.

A white man was riding his horse.
He heard a baby crying in the bush.
He came to the big log and listened.
He saw the pale feet of the baby sticking out.
He took the child and reared it and gave it
his name. And that baby was my mother.

Me? I'm Billy Bamboo. Anyone will tell you.
The buckjump rider, the bare knuckle fighter.
We used to stand toe to toe. We'd go down
to the creek and wash the blood off our faces
and come back and into it again. I was a flash
young feller in jodhpurs, riding boots and hat.

No, I can't see as well as I used to,
and I have to get about with this stick now.
You should have seen the old people. They would
have told you what the emu told the kangaroo.
Those old people are all gone from this mission.
They're all ghosts walking around in this place.

Adam Cooper
Related by Walter Blakeney, Wallaga Lake

Adam Cooper
was the cleverest blackfellow
God put on this earth.
He used to make
boomerangs.
He'd get his stone tomahawk
and cut out a circle in the ground.
In his circle he'd put
stringybark.
He'd throw his boomerang
and make it spin in the air
over the bark.
Up out of that stringybark
smoke would start to rise.
That stringybark would come
alight.
That's how this blackfellow
could make fire.

He'd send that boomerang
far away.
It would fall on the ground.
He'd clap his hands
and that boomerang would travel to him
along the ground.

He'd make a good fire
and let it burn down
to glowing coals.
Then he'd corroboree on the coals
and there wouldn't be a mark
to show on his feet.

He had a white stone.
He had it planted.
He wouldn't tell anyone
where he kept it hidden.
He used to
sing this stone in the language
and make it rain,
and rain heavy.

Adam Cooper's tribe
used to make nets out of rushes.
They'd stretch the nets
across a big creek
to stop the ducks coming down.
They'd throw their boomerangs
whistling over the ducks
to drive them into the nets.
Those ducks,
flying low,
would hit the nets
and break their necks.

That's the truth,
that's the finish.
That's the way they did it
in the old times.
I've seen it done myself.

Rites of Passage

Related by Walter Blakeney, Wallaga Lake

A feller was handed a stone by an old feller:
'This is your totem I'm givin' you. Look after it
an' you'll find that whatever you want to do
you'll have no trouble in doin' it. Lose it, or
break it, an' you'll die.' It was a clever stone.
No one was to look at it or to catch hold of it.

Nobody knows. He never offered to say
how the stone came to be broken. But the day arrived
when he found the stone was broken in his pocket.

He came to his next of kin. Told 'em he'd die
because the stone was broken. 'Bury me
with the honey an' the porcupine. Put the honey
at my feet, an' the porcupine at my head.' Sure enough
he died the next day.

They were battlin' then
to find the honey an' the porcupine. When you see
a porcupine, he always covers his beak with his little
hands. By ticklin' his hind feet, he takes his hands
off his beak. That's when they kill him by tappin'
him on the beak.

The porcupine belonged here. He was
only to be killed by blackfellers. That's why he
always covers his beak with his little hands.

They got the wild honey — the honey in the comb.
He was buried at Tingha. An' why did they bury him
with the honey an' porcupine? Well, take
old Nguppy James. He was buried with his spears
an' nulla-nulla for fightin'. They put these
things into his grave — his wish when he was dyin'.

Jarrangulli
Related by Percy Mumbulla, Wallaga Lake

Hear that tree-lizard singin' out,
Jarrangulli.
He's singin' out for rain.
He's in a hole up in that tree.
He wants the rain to fill that hole right up
an' cover him with rain.
That water will last him till
the drought comes on again.

It's comin' dry when he sings out,
Jarrangulli.
He's sure to bring the rain.
That feller, he's the real rain-lizard.
He's just the same as them black cockatoos,
they're the fellers for the rain.

He's deadly poison. He's
Jarrangulli.
He'll bite you sure enough.
You climb that tree an' put your hand
over that hole, he'll bite you sure enough.
He's black an' painted with white stripes.
Jarrangulli.
He's singing' out for rain.

Ejenak, the Porcupine
Related by Percy Mumbulla, Wallaga Lake

This little porcupine, Ejenak, whistles
a little song when he's travelling.
He goes along. Perhaps he goes down
to the river to have a drink of water.
He walks around the beach listening
all the time for anyone walking. If anyone
is around he hears the sad squeak.
He goes in the river and walks underneath
the water looking for food. He comes out
on the other side and walks about.
He comes to a bulldog ants' nest. He pokes
his claws into the nest and bulldog ants
run out. He pokes out his little tongue
and licks 'em up and gets his tucker.

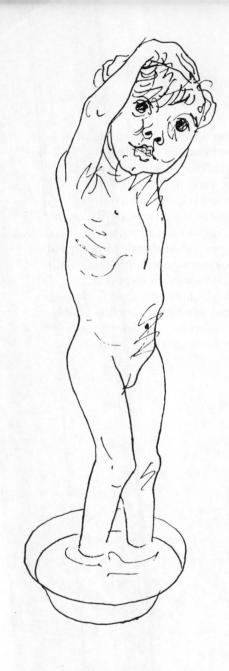

The Little People
Related by Percy Mumbulla, Wallaga Lake

Wathagundarls. They're the little people.
They live in the rocks an' caves at Tilba.
We don't interfere with them. You tread
on their corns an' they'll wale into you.
They'd get a stick an' knock you down,
tear the clothes off you an' drag you over
to the bulldogs' nest. You know them big
blue bulldog ants. They'd stir up them ants,
hold you over their nest an' sit on you
while the bulldogs bit you to death.

Them bulldogs don't hurt the little people.
Them ants are their *mudjingarls*, their spirits.
The little people don't understand clothes,
they're naked. They've got bows an' arrows.
They live on birds, that's what they hunt.
They never make a fire, that would
put them away. They eat their food raw an'
that's why they're so strong. They come out
in the evening, just about dark. Many a time
I've seen their little tracks in the dust.

Them Wathagundarls won't leave one another.
They do a Kelly together. They've got no
language, they only grunt. They're still here,
livin' wild in their own little wild state.

The Bugeen
Related by Percy Mumbulla, Wallaga Lake

You know, there's a *bugeen* around here.
He's after his 'meat'. He'll get him. He's
after some feller from the North Coast. I can't
talk too loud. He could be here, close,
watchin' us from out of the dark. Sammy Connolly
saw him over in the beans. He was pickin' an'
he looked up and saw the *bugeen* standin' up
in the ferns. He saw him down to the waist.
He was watchin' us pickin'. He had *jirral*[1] an' *walloo*.[2]

They saw the *bugeen* down at the shed. The
fellers was playin' cards, jackpot. They
saw this feller sneak into the shed. One feller
got a bottle an' went after him. But the *bugeen*
got away into the dark. When everything was quiet
he came back and stuck his head in the window
an' looked in. A woman spotted him, an' screamed.
He was as black as black. He ran away into the bush.
We never seen him since. But we can feel him.
He's here. He's after his 'meat'.

1 long hair
2 beard

32

The Whalers
Related by Percy Mumbulla, Wallaga Lake

My ole Uncle Brierly was the best whaler that ever
they seen in Twofold Bay. One mornin' they was
cuttin' up a whale, an' a killer whale came up
to where they were cuttin' up and jumped straight out
of the water an' splashed his tail, 'Pook-urr', on the water.

Soon as ever he seen this, ole Uncle sings out,
'*Reesh O.*' All the dark fellers run down an' jumped
into the whale-boat, all rowin' their hardest at
the big oars, great big long paddles. The killers was
swimmin' over one another, under and over
backwards an' forwards in front of the whale-boat, playin'.

They gets out an' sees the whale. Ole Uncle sings out,
'*Stern-a-moo!*' That means you have to get side on
to the whale. Ole Uncle gets the harpoon an' 'Boong!'
The harpoon goes into that monster an' kills him stone dead.

They towin' him in now, the killers swimming alongside,
playin' with the whale. The killers get real glad
whenever they see the dark fellers killin' a whale.

They comin' into the whalin' station now. They goin'
to chop the whale up an' boil him. They chuck a big
lump of blubber to the killer. He's like their dog.

The dark people would never go lookin' for whales. The killers
would let them know if there were whales about.
Ole Uncle would speak to them killers in the language.
They must have been *bugeens*, clever blackfellers.
They'd go as far as Narooma lookin' for whales.
Two would stop with the whale and one would go back
to Twofold Bay an' leap out of the water. 'Pook-urr!'
He'd slap his tail an' let the whalers know.

The killers would only tell the dark people.
The white people had to look for whales themselves.
It might be the middle of the night when the killers came.
You had no time to look for your trousers or shirt.
When ole Uncle sang out, '*Reesh O!*' you had to run
an' pile into that boat an' out. No matter
if the waves were as high as them trees,
you still had to go because you were signed on.

No shark would touch you with them killers there.
The killers would chop a shark to pieces. A sword-fish,
you know what he's like, he wouldn't have a chance.
An' a porpoise, he'd make a porpoise sweat he's so fast.

If the whale-boat was out of sight of land an' got
smashed, the killers was there. They would be swimmin'
round an' round, keepin' the sharks away.
If them killers seen a man gettin' tired, they would
swim underneath him, put a fin under his arm an'
hold him up until the launch came to pick him up.

The killers would be playin' all around the launch goin' back.

Arr, my old Uncle Brierly was a champ. They've got
his photo down at Twofold Bay. He'd never use
the harpoon-gun. He'd used the harpoon-spear.
He had a knack of killin' the whale, he'd put the harpoon
right into him an' kill the whale stone dead.

There's three whales, the sperm whale, the black whale,
an' the humper. A sperm whale can smash a boat with his tail,
an' come at you with his mouth open. He's got teeth.

The little killer would swim alongside the whale an'
soon as he opened his mouth, the little killer would go
inside and bite his tongue out, chew it right off.

Big Ben the killer was a wizard. Then there was Hookey
an' Big Tom. Soon as ever the dark people left
Twofold Bay an' come to Wallaga Lake, them killers
went north, because there were no blackfellers there.

Ole Mrs Davidson, her husband was the boss of the
whalin' station at Boyd Town, she could have told you.

Uncle Abraham, Whose Blackfeller's Name was Minah
Related by Percy Mumbulla, Wallaga Lake

1. *Guneena*
Every time I lie down alongside a river
and hear the wind in the oaks
it puts me in mind of my poor old grand-uncle Minah.

My old grand-uncle was lying down under the oaks
and he was dying. My old dad was with him.
My old dad could feel these things. He had that power.

He said, 'I think I'll shift you.
I don't like it here.
There's something going to happen.'

He shifted old uncle Minah,
put the tent-sticks in another place.
It wasn't very long before a big limb broke off
and fell down and stuck in the ground
where my grand-uncle had been lying.

And my old father brought him back to die
at Wallaga Lake.
He'd been caught with the *guneena*,
the devil's stones.

When I'm lying down under these oaks
down at Bega
I used to think about poor old uncle Minah.
He used to put his arms round me and say,
'My great-great-grandchildren.'

I was his favourite.
I was like a little poddy calf,
a little fat-belly feller, you might say.
I was never with the young fellers.

I followed the old people.
They would hunt me back,
I would cry and they would take me up
and put me on their shoulders.
I used to sit down and listen
to the old people yarning.

But these young fellers, they don't realise.
They'd laugh at you.
They say, 'Ar, he's a *burra*, a liar.
He couldn't catch a dorg with such things.'
But those things did happen.

2.   *Marrung*
Whenever I used to see one of those old fellers
going off with a spear for *marrung* — fish —
I'd watch him. I'd run after him.

The old lad would crouch right down with his spear.
He'd make a faint move to frighten the fish.
When the fish didn't move
he'd drive the spear right into him.
He'd have that fish shaking on his spear.

I was only a little feller
but I had that sense to follow
and learn how to do all those things.
That's why I don't use a line for my fish.
I use my fish-spear;
my father taught me how to make them.
I can use the woomera and the spear with two barbs.
I can make a boomerang to go whistling like a duck
and come back,
right back to my foot.

Every time I come to a river like this
and hear the wind in those she-oaks
I sit down and those times come back to me.
I can see my old great-uncle Minah lying down.
He had a long white smoky beard, *walloo* we call it,
and his hair, *jirral*, was smoke-dried, white.

He was lying down and looking at the sky
and must have been saying in his own language
'I'm leaving all my little grandchildren.
I'm leaving them.'

3.   *Muleemah*
One time all our people travelled
from Wallaga Lake to Bermagui to play cricket.
Uncle Abraham was the last one to arrive.
While he was travelling he saw a woman on the road.
This woman was a *muleemah*,
a man dressed in women's clothes.

Uncle Abraham said to himself,
'It's a *bugeen*.'

He goes round the back of this *muleemah*
and comes out onto the road again.
As he is walking along the road
he sees this *muleemah* again in front of him
walking along in women's clothes.
Again Uncle Abraham goes round
and gets past this *muleemah*.
When he gets to Bermagui he tells everyone
that he was caught by a *muleemah*.

Uncle Abraham plays cricket
and his side wins the game.
Then they all go back to Wallaga Lake.
There Uncle Abraham gets sick.

4.   *Doonoots*

Old Jacky (Mumbulla, my father) travels
with Uncle Abraham to Mosquito Point,
the two old-men put up their camp there.
Old Jacky makes a fire and all the *doonoots*,
the mopokes, call out:
> No sleep, no smoke,
> no sleep, no smoke,
> gook-gook, gook-gook.

The *doonoots* were calling out
and killing Uncle Abraham.
They were tying up his guts.
The old-man was dying.
Old Jacky put more wood on the fire
but the mopokes flew up
and perched on the camp-poles.
> Gook-gook, gook-gook,
> no sleep, no smoke,
> gook-gook, gook-gook,

they called out.

Old Jacky grabbed the fire-sticks
and pelted them at the mopokes.
He knocked one of the birds
down from the camp-poles.
He picked the mopoke up
and chucked him in the fire to burn alive
and to stop the mopokes
from killing the old feller.

But all night until daylight
the *doonoots* sing out:
> Gook-gook, gook-gook,
> no sleep, no smoke,
> gook-gook, gook-gook.

When daylight comes the poor old-man
had passed away in the mia-mia camp.
They took him away and buried him
and saw him no more.

Billy Bulloo
Related by Percy Mumbulla, Wallaga Lake

Old Billy Bulloo was a clever old man.
He had three wives.
He'd never go out fishin' on a calm day.
But if the sea was rough — mountains
high — he'd jump in his canoe
an' get his fish by spearin' 'em.

A mullet, he never travels in the calm.
He waits for the wind to blow a gale.
Soon as ever he feels that wind on him —
cold — he jumps out of the water.
He's feelin' for that westerly wind.
When that wind blows you see the water
black with leapin' mullet, thousands
an' thousands of leaping mullet:
that's when old Billy Bulloo used to get his fish.

Old Billy Bulloo found the gold
on the Shoalhaven. He'd go
to the publican in Nowra an' trade his gold
for tucker or a bottle of rum.
Lots of white men tried to foller him up.
But when he got to the bush he'd lose 'em.

The last of my people he told
was my old granny.
While she was in her health an' strength,
she wanted to take us out an' show us
where it was. But you know
what young fellers is — they're here
today an' gone tomorrer.

The Surprise Attack

Related by Percy Mumbulla, Wallaga Lake

Old Fred Freeman was tellin' me about
the time the Red-Hill tribe was cleaned right out.
All the old hands, they was asleep like, see;
an' this other tribe sneaked up on 'em from tree
to tree, an' caught 'em all asleep an' teared
into 'em with their boomerangs an' spears.

Boomerangs, they teared through bone an' gristle.
When they drove them boomerangs they made 'em whistle.
The Red-Hill tribe, they couldn't make a break,
They grabbed their boomerangs an', half awake,
blazed back at 'em till all around,
men stuck through with spears lay on the ground.

You couldn't pull them barbed spears from inside
a man. You'd drag his guts out if you tried,
said old Fred Freeman, tellin' me about
the time the Red-Hill tribe was cleaned right out.

Captain Cook

Related by Percy Mumbulla, Wallaga Lake

Tungeei, that was her native name.
she was a terrible tall woman
who lived at Ulladulla.
She had six husbands,
an' buried the lot.

She was over a hundred, easy,
when she died.
She was tellin' my father,
they were sittin' on the point
that was all wild scrub.

The big ship came and anchored
out at Snapper Island.
He put down a boat
an' rowed up the river
into Bateman's Bay.

He landed on the shore of the river,
the other side from where the
church is now.
When he landed he gave the Kurris clothes,
an' those big sea-biscuits.
Terrible hard biscuits they was.

When they were pullin' away to go back
to the ships, these wild Kurris
were runnin' out of the scrub.
They'd stripped right off again.
They were throwin' the clothes an' biscuits
back at Captain Cook
as his men were pullin' away in the boat.

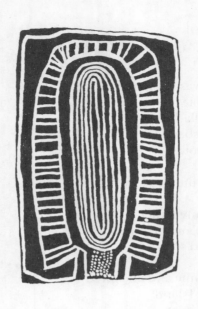

Lake Carjelligo

The Rainbow Snake
Related by Fred Biggs, Ngeamba tribe

Warwai — that's a very big snake in the river, or out in the lake. He goes out wherever there's a big lot of water. He's a big feller. He'll swallow you. He's not about now. I think that the old people must have shut him up.

In the 'seventy' flood, Warwai went out to the Nine Mile Lake, that's what the white man calls it. It's nine miles to Canoble Station. That Warwai, he went right out in the water. While Warwai was alive that lake would never have gone dry.

My old people used to get their rations from Canoble Station. They used to walk round this lake, about thirty miles. They got this rations for helping to keep the rabbits down. Well, one old feller, he started out one day to go to the station for his rations.

He came to a bit of land that crossed the end of the lake. He went across this bit of land and got his rations at the station. He was coming back late in the afternoon. Well, this Warwai had come down the lake and was lying in the shallow water sunning himself.

This old feller, he thought that Warwai was that red ground. Of course, he was a fair age, that old feller was, but he was clever. Well, he put his foot on that Warwai, he walked right on top of him. And that Warwai, he reared up and swallowed that old feller, rations and all.

Well when that old feller found that he was swallowed, he was a *wirreengum*, a clever-feller, he busted that snake right open and walked out of him. He got up and walked away and left that Warwai there. He never even got wet and he saved his rations.

That Warwai died there. The bones were there for years. A lot of old people told me about them. When I saw the bones they were crumbling. If you didn't know, you'd think they were bullock bones. They were as round as that old wagon tyre. They must have been there for years until they crumbled right away. We were looking at them twenty or thirty years back. They were the bones of Warwai all right.

If that Warwai hadn't been killed that lake could never have dried up. It would have been for everlasting.

The Child who had no Father
Related by Fred Biggs, Ngeamba tribe

Before the white man came here with his sheep,
the plains were covered with all kinds of flowers.
Two sisters would go walking through the flowers
looking for any food that they could find.
And when those sisters walked among the flowers,
there were no *mai*, no men, in all the world.

One evening, as one sister walked along,
she saw one flower and stooped and broke it off.
Inside, the flower looked like a baby's face.
She got two bits of bark and put the flower
between them, underneath a log. She thought
no more about it and walked on through the flowers.

This sister came again one evening, 'Oh, more
and more this flower has a baby's face.'
She took some possum fur and wrapped it round
the flower and laid it underneath the log.
Next evening when this sister came to find
the flower she found a baby sleeping there.

She found her breasts had milk and, every evening,
she went out through the flowers and fed the child.
Her sister saw her sister's breasts had formed.
'Oh, you must have a baby.' 'Yes.' 'Oh where?'
'Out there among the flowers.' The sisters went
and found the child and brought it to their cave.

That child became a wise and clever man
and, afterwards, he went up into the sky.
And always, when I hear the white men preaching,
this story comes into my mind. That child,
he was like Jesus. He came into the world
without a father. He was formed from a flower.

47

That woman touched that flower. If she had not plucked that flower, this could not have happened.

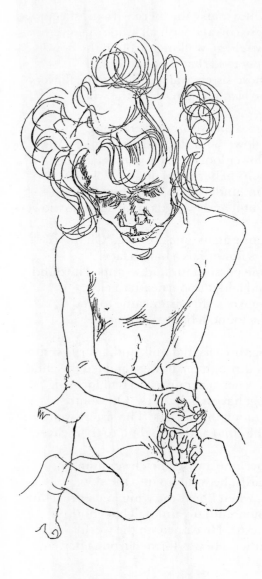

Mapooram

Related by Fred Biggs, Ngeamba tribe

Go out and camp somewhere. You're lying down.
A wind comes, and you hear this *Mapooram*.
'What's that?' you say. Why, that's a *Mapooram*.
You go and find that tree rubbing itself.
It makes all sorts of noises in the wind.
·It might be like a sheep, or like a cat
or like a baby crying, or someone calling,
a sort of whistling-calling when the wind
comes and swings and rubs two boughs like that.

A *wirreengun*, a clever-feller, sings
that tree. He hums a song, a *Mapooram*:
a song to close things up, or bring things out,
a song to bring a girl, a woman from that tree.
She's got long hair, it falls right down her back.
He's got her for himself. He'll keep her now.

One evening, it was sort of rainy-dark,
they built a mia-mia, stripping bark.
You've been out in the bush sometime and seen
them old dry pines with loose bark coming off.
You get a lot of bark from those old dry pines,
before they rot and go too far, you know.
That woman from the tree, she pulled that bark.
It tore off, up and up the tree. It pulled
her up, into the tree, up, up into the sky.
Well, she was gone. That was the end of it.
No more that *wirreengun* could call her back.

'*Mapooram. Mapooram.*' 'What's that?' you say.
Why, that's two tree boughs rubbing in the wind.

49

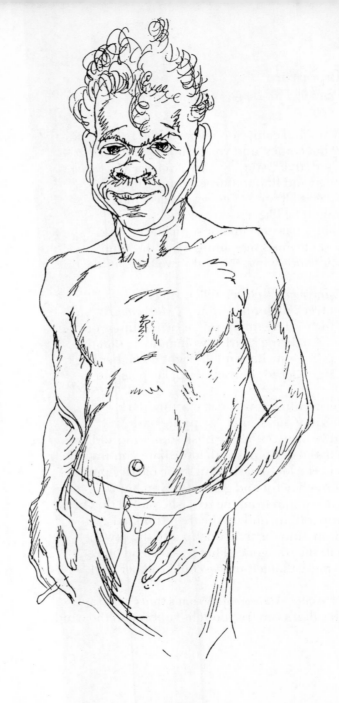

The Star-Tribes
Related by Fred Biggs, Ngeamba tribe

Look, among the boughs. Those stars are men.
There's Ngintu, with his dogs, who guards the skins
of Everlasting Water in the sky.
And there's the Crow-man, carrying on his back
the wounded Hawk-man. There's the Serpent, Thurroo,
glistening in the leaves. There's Kapeetah,
the Moon-man, sitting in his mia-mia.

And there's those Seven Sisters travelling
across the sky. They make the real cold frost.
You hear them when you're camped out on the plains.
They look down from the sky and see your fire
and, 'Mai, mai, mai!' they sing out as they run
across the sky. And, when you wake, you find
your swag, the camp, the plains, all white with frost.

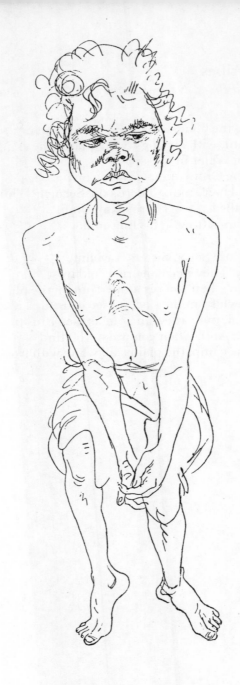

Brewarrina

Biggie Billa, the Porcupine
Related by Maria Boney, Yoalari tribe

My old mother told me this story. There was one old
man, a grandfather, and he had two little grandsons.
This old grandfather he'd kill a porcupine. He'd send
the two poor little fellers out to get some leaves,
coolibah leaves, to cook in a ground oven with
the porcupine. The two little grandsons would
set out. They'd call out, *'Nguga Thaththa?'*
That means, 'Here, Grandfather?' But the grandfather
would tell them to run further on.

And while these two poor little fellers were right away
huntin' for those leaves, that old grandfather, I suppose,
would eat nearly all of the porcupine.

Just the same, if that old grandfather had emu
or kangaroo, he'd do the same thing, send them
two little poor fellers out while he ate up all the tucker.

So anyway, one day all the people from roundabout
found out what this old feller was doing.

And these two little boys, they seen all these butterflies
comin'. You know how they all go past, all
driftin' past. The two little boys would see
the butterflies were people with spears comin'
after that old grandfather. The two little boys
would call out, *'Thaththa!* You see all the people comin'?'
And that old grandfather he would say, 'O,
they're not people, they're butterflies.'

They came then. Them butterfly people got to
that old grandfather because he was cruel to
the boys. They got to him with their spears.

All those spears bin stick into that old grandfather.
That old grandfather, he became a porcupine.
He been porcupine ever since. And I suppose
all the butterfly people took them two little
boys away with them and reared them up.

Garnee and Gillarr

Related by Maria Boney, Yoalari tribe

I don't know what these two young fellers was fightin'
about. There was two young fellers. They had a fight.

This Garnee, the frill necked lizard, he threw a
boomerang and hit the other feller that was fightin'.

One feller that was fightin' was a gillarr and the
other was a garnee.

If ever you pluck a gillarr you'll see his head
flat on the top where the boomerang hit. And that's
the blood that fell off his head that made his breast red.

Then this Gillarr who got hit by a boomerang, he
chased the Garnee and rubbed him in the bindi-eyes,
those big roly-poly bushes and burrs. That's how
the garnee came to get those sharp things all over him.

You can't catch a hold of him, they'll stick into you.
And that's how the garnee came to be like that.

Dinnawin and Burralga

Related by Maria Boney, Yoalari tribe

There was an emu and a native-companion.
They were mates, and they used to feed about together.
And one day this emu said, 'Hey, why don't you
get rid of some of those little ones of yours? We'd
have a good feed then.' This emu is talking.
He had his little ones planted in the grass and scrub.

So this native-companion did away with a lot
of his children. And only two were left. Then this
native-companion, he started to cry. He was sorry
about the little ones, see. You hear them native-
companions sing out, they make a terrible noise.

While the native-companion was crying, this emu,
he went and brought all his young ones out. He
put his wing out and he ran round the native companion
with all his little ones. This old emu, he was
getting flash and runnin' round with his wing
out and showing off all his children.

Ah, but the native-companion was sorry then.
But he said to himself, 'I'll catch him.'

So the native-companion left it until the emu
had forgotten all about the trick he had played.

Then one day the native-companion said,
'Ah, I know what we'll do. We'll cut our wing
now so that we can have a decent feed. He said
to the emu, 'We'll get a good pick.' So anyway,
the emu, he cut his wing. But the native companion,
he didn't cut his. He flew round the emu, telling
the emu what he could do. '*Ngurroo gulgai!*'
he called. That means 'I've got arms to fly

56

about with!' The native-companion, he showed
that emu what he could do.

But I don't know what that old emu said. He couldn't
say nothing. He'd cut his arms. He'd only got
short arms. That's why, when you see the native-
companion, he's got only two little ones. But when
you find that emu's nest, he's got a lot of little ones.

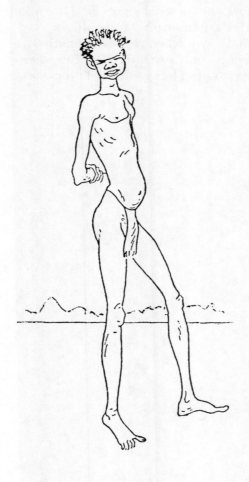

New South Wales North Coast

The Sandpiper
Related by Mary Turnbull, Bunjalung tribe

When we were children we used to gather *gippaiuns*,
they're like wild strawberries that grow in the bush,
and always we'd hear this sorrowful, wandering call
travelling away through the scrub by the edge of the sea.
Running along the sand was a little bird,
stopping and running again at the edge of the waves
with a sorrowful call in the wind and roar of the sea.

I remember asking my mother about that bird,
and she told us how it had lost its little one.
It might have been a thousand years since that woman,
whose spirit is now a bird, first lost her son.
It's a summery bird. It comes in the summer-time.
My mother, she told us the story, but somehow it's gone
with the time we gathered the *gippaiuns* in the bush.

When you're going along the beach you'll see that bird.
It will run right up and have a look at you.
She's in trouble, you see. She makes that sorrowful call.
She's crying and searching still for her little one.

The Platypus
Related by Dick Donnelly, Bunjalung tribe

Djanbun's the platypus. He was once a man.
He came out of Washpool Creek, the old people said.
Djanbun's travelling, a firestick in his hand,
across the big mountains to the Clarence River.
He's blowing on the firestick to make it flame.
But it won't flame and whenever the sparks
fall down from the firestick they turn to gold.

This platypus man's mouth starts to get wide
from blowing on the firestick. We used to blow
on the firestick when we were young. My mother
used to say to us, 'Don't blow on the firestick
like that or you'll be like Djanbun the platypus.'

When Djanbun gets down to the Clarence River,
he's got a big mouth from blowing on the firestick.
He starts to wonder, 'What am I going to do now?'
So he throws the firestick down and he thinks,
'I'll jump into the water.' As soon as he jumps
in the water, he turns into a platypus. That's him,
that's Djanbun now. He was a man one time.

Now Billie Charlie, he found this nugget of gold
at the place where Djanbun jumped into the water.
When I heard about this, I thought, 'Well now,
that's the firestick he found.' Because he found
that gold where the firestick was thrown down.

The old people told me this story. They showed me
the way Djanbun went across the mountain range.

The Frog who was King
Related by Tom Whaddy, Gumbangirr tribe

This happened at Grassy Heads. This happened when
the world was made, years and years ago.

There was an old man, an old king he was.
He used to look after Australia, we'll say.
Then one day another old feller came from the other
side of the world. Where would he come from,
Africa? That's where the lions and tigers are.

He came across to Grassy Heads and asked this
old king did he have any lions and tigers in
Australia. 'Yes', said the old king, 'we've got
all those things here.' He was telling a lie.
He didn't want those animals here.

Well, the old feller goes back to wherever he
came from. He came back with a tiger. That's
deadly, isn't it? He asks the old king again,
'Have you got anything like this here?'
The old king says, '*Yoo, ngunee kunee walkung.*'
That means, 'Yes, we've got all those things here.'

At last the old feller from the other side
got sick of bringing these animals over, he was
bringing them over one after another. So he cursed
the old king: '*Tsure ninga ngang yatanga!*'
That means he turned the old king into a frog,
them big brown fellers. That big brown frog says,
'Wark, wark, wark. *Ngunee kunee walkung. Gityeeng
Boseeya.*' This means 'O we don't want anything
like that. We've got 'em here in this place.'

This old feller picked up the old king and threw
him down into a crevice in the rocks, and that's

61

where he is to this day. Because he told a lie. But he saved Australia from these deadly animals.

So now we've got all the quiet animals, kangaroos, emus, wallabies, possums, and all that — except the crocodile. That old feller must have sneaked him in.

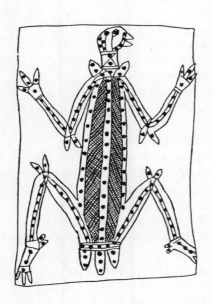

The Man who Killed the Porpoise
Related by Bob Turnbull

In the wintertime, the tribes all along this coast used to camp
in the hills and caves in the mountains where there was plenty
of firewood and plenty of tucker, wallaby, porcupine, possum
and all that.

Summertime, they'd make down to the beaches for a feed
of fish. They'd change their food. That's when they'd get the
porpoises to help them.

The porpoises were the old people's friends. When the
season of the sea-mullet was in, the old people would go down
to the river and beat their spears on the water. The school of
porpoises would come and chase the schools of sea-mullet
right into the shallow water, ankle deep, where the old people
used to get just enough for two or three meals without wasting any. The old people used to tell us that when we went fish-
ing we should spear just enough fish for our needs, without
wasting any.

Another thing, when the old people wanted to cross the
river in canoes, or by swimming across, the porpoises would
always be there to chase away the sharks.

The old people used to make a little net out of kurrajong
bark. They'd go down to the beach and beat the water. They'd
call on the porpoises. All the porpoises would come and chase
the fish into the bay. Then the old people would shoot the net
around the fish and catch them.

One day, two men went down to the beach with their net.
They got too greedy. When they ran the net around the fish,
they got a porpoise in it. One of these fellers was curious
about this porpoise. He wanted to know how it came to be so
clever. Well, out of curiosity, he killed the porpoise and cut it
open on the beach.

A good while after this, some of the people of another tribe
went down to the beach to net some fish. They beat on the
water, they called to the porpoises, they sang them, but the
porpoises wouldn't appear.

Those people couldn't get any fish. They wondered what was the matter. They couldn't make out why the porpoises had let them down.

They thought to themselves, 'There's something wrong.' They went to the oldest man of the tribe. They wanted to know why the porpoises wouldn't come to hunt the fish for them.

Well, this old-man went to see another old-man, one belonging to the tribe whose fisherman had killed the porpoise. These two old-men met and talked together. 'Well,' said this second old-man, 'I don't know anything about it, but I'll find out.'

This old-man soon found out that one of his men had killed a porpoise when he had caught it in the net.

They took this feller who had killed the porpoise and killed him with a boomerang. They used the boomerang like a tomahawk to kill him. Then they took this man and threw him into the sea and threw the boomerang in after him.

That man, when he was thrown into the sea, turned into a porpoise. Next time when you see a porpoise jumping and turning over, you have to look, you'll see a boomerang on his side.

Killing this feller did no good. It didn't make the porpoises come back.

Those two tribes had a fight over the killing of that porpoise, but it still didn't do any good. From that time the porpoises would never help those people with the fish no more. No matter how they called on the porpoises to come and help them, the porpoises stopped coming.

They never came back no more.

Gineevee, the Black Swan
Related by Ken Gordon, Bunjalung tribe

Old Mick Robertson could have told you about the stars,
every star you can see in the sky. He had names for them all.
The stars must have been his *jurraveel* because he could tell
you all about them.

He told me that the Southern Cross is Gineevee, that is the
black swan flying along. And the two pointers are the head
and the tail of a spear thrown by a blackfeller to kill
Gineevee.

The Southern Cross only came here with the white man.
Before the white man came he was a swan.
That's a *jurraveel*. You won't see Gineevee in any other
part of the world.

The Brolga

Related by James McGrath, Ngumbarr tribe

There was a man.
He was a *birroogan*,
a real pretty feller.
He was like God, see.
This *birroogan* was out in the bush
and his *ngudgeehullum*,
his brother-in-law, killed him.
The brother-in-law was
a *ngaloongirr*,
a clever-feller.
He chopped the body
of the *birroogan* up
then put all the parts
of the body together again
and sang the body.
He made the body as though
it was alive again.
But the *birroogan* was really
a dead man.

There was a war on.
This *birroogan* had to be killed in the war.
He had to be killed
to pay back the death
of a man in another tribe.
The *birroogan* got up
and went back to the camp.
He said to his mother
'I'm going to the war now.'
Then he hung up his dilly-bag
that held all his belongings
in the camp.
He said to his mother
'If this dilly-bag falls down

you will know I am dead.'
So his mother waited in the camp
while the war was on
and the dilly-bag fell down.

The *birroogan*
was right back in the fight.
He was just watching.
One of the other tribe
was looking for the *birroogan*.
At last he saw him.
This man threw a spear
right up to where the *birroogan* was standing.
The spear sang through the air
and hit the *birroogan* in the chest.
Then all the warriors sang out
'It is finished. *Birroogan* is dead.'

Then the man who had speared the *birroogan* said
to all the warriors
'you can all turn into tea-trees now.'
And there's thousands of tea-trees in that place
all twisted and bent with outflung arms.

Then the man who had speared the *birroogan* said
'I'll turn into a hawk.'
That hawk is *ngudeegullum*.
He's a man-eater.

The mother of the *birroogan* said
'I'll turn into a brolga
and I'm going to see my son now.'
So every evening the brolga
goes to the grave of her son
the *birroogan*
and dances around his grave at Arracoon
near South West Rocks on the Macleay River
near the entrance to Trial Bay.

That *birroogan* has a rock there
where he was buried.
It's still there.
It's at the Arracoon Racecourse near South West Rocks.

The Aboriginal Jesus
Related by John Flanders, Gumbangirr tribe

Before ever the white man was on the world, God had two
sons. Them two sons travelled the world dragging a vine
behind them. They made the rivers and the headlands. One
of the brothers was called *Birroogun. Birroogun* is our Jesus.

Our brother went round by the coast. The other feller went
right round the other side of the world. These two brothers
met at the Gulf of Carpentaria.

One said, 'Now, brother, I'm going to stay here forever.' No
aeroplane with a woman in it can fly over that place, the wind
will drive it away. No ship at all can go there, it will sink if it
does. The water boils and whirlpools form. The power of that
place will sink the ship.

The brother who went along the coast came to Smoky
Cape, between Kempsey and Macksville. He found an old
woman and her grand-daughter there. The girl was feeding a
little eel in a spring. The old woman said, 'I'll go and see what
she's feeding with them grubs.'

She found it was an eel nearly as big as herself. She went
back to the camp and made a spear. 'I'll go and kill that eel
and eat it,' she said. She speared the eel. The eel was so big the
spear broke. The eel went right through the mountains by the
sea.

Everyone goes through that hole round on to the rocks
when they go snapper-fishing.

When the brother was going along the beach, he saw that
eel. He dragged it along with him. He took it to the old
woman and said, 'Now, you'd better come to Smoky Cape to
the tribe.'

There were thousands of wild people. My mother was half
wild. All the white people and the black police shot them.
People won't believe it today. I've argued with the police
sergeant here at Bowraville about it.

When that brother dragged the eel, he left those tea-trees
growing apart when he went through. They talk about Jesus

feeding the people with the three fishes, this *Birroogun* fed thousands of wild blackfellers with that one eel.

He went from there to the Macleay River. All the black-fellers went with him. He took the intestines out of a *dungirr*, a koala bear. He left the bear alive on the tree. He made a bridge out of those intestines and they all went across on that bridge, and there were thousands of sharks waiting underneath in the water for anyone to fall in.

Old goanna wanted to cut that bridge with a stone-axe so that some of them would fall in the river. But *Birroogun*, our Jesus, wouldn't let him.

Old goanna got left behind. He couldn't see the *Birroogun* and the *Birroogun* had made the bridge disappear. Old goanna had to stay behind.

The *Birroogun* and all the people camped. He told this old woman,

> 'Now I'm going to hang up my dilly-bag
> in this tree.
> If this dilly-bag falls down
> you'll know that they've killed me.'

> The *Birroogun* went to Arracoon
> Where the racecourse is now.
> When the people saw him
> they came with their spears.
> That is the battle-field
> where the grandstand is today.
> They said,
> 'We want this feller.
> He's travelled the world.'

> They speared him at the place
> where the winning-post is.
> He's got a grave there.
> And two brolgas corroboreed on that grave
> for years.

They kept it clean
never let any grass grow on it.

Some white feller went there
and shot them two brolgas
long ago.
Them birds don't do any harm.
You'll see them.
They corroboree.

You'll hear them, they sing out
'Kirr-irr-irr.'
They're chuckin' their spears up in the air
and catching them.
The warriors carried the *Birroogun*
on their spears to this place
and buried him.

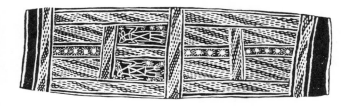

The Battle of the Birds
Related by Alec Vesper, Gullibul tribe

This story is about Jigai. He's the cat-bird.
If you heard him singing out in the scrub,
you'd swear it was a baby crying.

There was a man called Mamugun. He's the
green pigeon now. Mamugun had made many
boomerangs, and there was a tribe who came
on him as he was sleeping.

The tribe saw the boomerangs lying beside Mamugun.
'Look', they said, 'see his boomerangs? Steal
them while he's asleep!' So they stole Mamugun's boomerangs.

They went out into a clear space. They started
throwing the boomerangs all about. Mamugun
woke up and found that his boomerangs were all gone.

He went after the men to get them back.
He saw these men throwing both his left-hand
boomerangs and his right-hand boomerangs,
playing about with them.

Mamugun told these men that the boomerangs
were his but these men ignored him. At last
they said, 'These are ours now!' So Mamugun
started mourning for his boomerangs. Then, as
the men kept on throwing them, the boomerangs
kept on going out towards the sea. There they turned
into swifts — you know, those birds that dart about.

And this Mamugun was weeping very much.
All the other birds, such as the lyre-birds, the
regent birds, the black fishtail birds and the

rifle-birds, all the birds of the scrub, were concerned
with what he was crying about.

Mamugun was weeping to all the birds that
his boomerangs were stolen.
All the birds were deeply concerned about
Mamugun weeping. And they asked him what was
the cause of his weeping. And he said, 'All my
boomerangs have been stolen by the people.'
'*Gunnarra Yenda*!' the birds cried.
'Throw out a challenge to have a war at a certain place!'
Mamugun agreed and told them to send
a messenger. So the birds sent a messenger
to say that war was declared.

At their own camp they beat the shield with a
nulla-nulla first to let all the tribes know
'*Gunnarra yenden beh*!' That means, 'We have
declared war!' So all the birds declared war
against the *Borrgorrgin*, that's the sea-faring people.
When these messengers were sent, as I've told you
in another story, they hit their shields and
sang out, '*Deerr*!' That's like a bugle call,
a war-cry.

So they got ready on both sides, and the tribe
of Jigai was also told; and they came to assist
Mamugun. And the war started in the afternoon
about three o'clock, and the main battle was on the
following day, and the third day's battle was for
the championship, and that was fought in couples.

And this Jigai then, he was a *buloogun*, a
well built, good looking man. He was hurt in
the fight with the champion. In this battle, Jigai
received the hurt which caused his death. So
both sides came to a term of peace and stopped
the battle.

Just before Jigai gave up the ghost he
said, 'Bury me on the top of the mountain.'
And they took him to Jigai, that's his own
place. And as they prepared the top of the mountain
for his grave, as the corpse was laying down
he sang out 'Jigai!' And they said, 'He
doesn't want to be buried here.'

They carried him to the next mountain
called Boorabee, that's the name of the native bear.
And as they had the place ready, he sang out 'Jigai!' again.

They took him to Wathumbil Mountain. They prepared
a place, had it all levelled out, and they
thought, 'This is the place where we're going to
bury him.' All the birds were talking among
themselves because Jigai was keeping quiet
at last. Then, when they were just about to
sink the grave, he called out 'Jigai!' again.

They took him to another mountain. This
is now Jigai Mountain, which is called Mount
Lion. It is approaching the Loop and Loop
of the Brisbane-Sydney railway. The birds
there prepared the place for Jigai's burial.
They sank the grave and buried him. This tomb
is there to this day to be seen by anyone
who goes to the top of the mountain.

There's a cleared space on the mountain-top
with stones all round. Then all the birds
went back to their own tribal places. They all
belong to the Main Scrub, the coastal scrub
we call *Woorbeh*.

The Song of the Vine
Related by Charlotte Williams, Githavul tribe

There was a vine whose spirit was a
man. These forest vines, they were the
spirit peoples' vines. They were not
made by men. And someone cut this
vine and there this man is struggling
to be alive. This is my own grandfather's song.

'I am here,' the song says, 'I am this vine.
My life is going away from me, from this
ground, this place, this dust. My ears are
ringing. Gaungun the spirit-woman is
making my ears no good. My ears are
ringing. I'll never see this world no more.'

And one man came along and saw this vine
struggling to be alive. He covered it with
dust. When I think of my old people how
they would sit down and sing their songs
to me, I could cry . . .

The Song of Darmunjura
Related by Dick Donnelly, Bunjalung tribe

Billy Nickel reared me up. We got so fond of one another. We used to sing these songs together under a gum-tree. He was a great singer, was Billy Nickel. This is the song of the gold-*jurraveel*.

You see, out near Baryulgil, there's two mountains, Yillin and Darmunjura. Billy Nickel knew that on Darmunjura there was a gold-*jurraveel*. One day, he thought, 'I'll go and get this gold.' He was a *maragun*, that's an initiated man.

Anyhow, Billy Nickel went up on the mountain. I was grubbing out stumps at the time. Billy Nickel was on a cliff and there was a creek flowing there. He was looking for the gold. He was just starting to part the long weeds flowing in the water when the mountain started to crack, the mountain started to growl.

The mountain was up against Billy Nickel for interfering with those weeds. The mountain spoke to him. It said, 'You have interfered with this *jurraveel*. You don't belong here. You belong in the Bunjalung tribe.'

Billy Nickel went back to his blady-grass camp. He was lying on the blady-grass outside his *bunguin*, his humpy made of branches and grass. Blady-grass was given to us by God. He got a dream. When he woke, he says to his wife, Susan, 'I see these two women, the *gaungun*.' Those two spirit-women, the *gaungun*, were haunting him, they were tormenting him.

His wife Susan said, 'You had no right going up on to that mountain and interfering with that *jurraveel*.'

Next night these two women showed themselves in a dream again to Billy Nickel. He saw them coming to haunt him. His wife, Susan, was wondering what would happen to her husband. She was rousing on him.

Anyhow, those two *gaungun* kept on haunting Billy Nickel until he went blind. When he was blind, he sat down under that gum-tree. He had his two *djalgai*, his song-sticks. All is quiet. He sings.

76

He came to me. He said, 'I've made up a song. Listen to me.' He was a nice man. I missed him when he died. This is the song of Darmunjura that I caught from Billy Nickel.

'What shall I do? What shall I do?
The mountain Darmunjura has wrestled with me.
Back there on the mountain, I thought the gold
was in the water. Soon as I pulled those weeds,
the mountain started to crack, the mountain started
to rumble.
I pulled only those weeds, but the mountain was
offended.
Hold me now. The mountain has wrestled with me.
What am I going to do? You've got to hold me.
You've got to keep me. You've got to guide me now.'

The Myth of the Mountain
Related by Eustan Williams, Githabul tribe

Look at that mountain Jalgumbun standing up,
see how it goes straight up on all its sides.
No man can climb that mountain. Look at its head,
through the mist, covered with trees. I worked
as chainman to Phinney MacPherson, the surveyor,
right along this range and, when we come
to Jalgumbun, he says to me, 'Now Eustan,
let me see them steps you say are cut
out in this mountain.' And as I pointed out
them steps, he stood there, writing in his notebook
the story of the mountain that I told him.

That mountain Jalgumbun was once a tree.
A man went after honey in that tree.
He climbed up with the vine-rope round himself
and round the tree. And as he climbed he cut
footholds with his stone-axe. And his wives
were waiting in the forest down below.

'Where are you?' they called out. And he called back,
'I'm chopping out the honey.' Then these women
wanted to come up closer, but again
the man sang out, 'No, wait there where you are,'
and went on chopping, chopping out the honey.
At last he called out, 'Here it is,' and rolled
the piece of wood with all the honey in it
down to the butt and big roots of the tree.
They sat down in their camp and ate that honey,
and travelled then away along the range.

That night there was no moon. The women looked
out into the night and whispered together.
'Oh, look what is that "something" over there?,'
'Oh, it's like a shadow.' 'See, that "something"'

over there is blocking out the stars.'
And in the morning when they woke they saw
the mountain that was never there before,
Jalgumbun standing up against the sky.

Well, there's a tree called Jalgumbun that grows
here in the ranges. It has a real soft skin.
The fellers from the mill at Urbenville
come with their axes, tractors, and their gear,
and fell and lop them trees and drag them
out from the ranges of their native home.

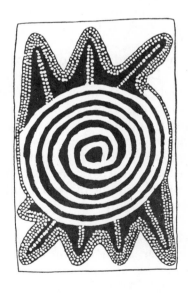

Dirrangun at Tooloom

Related by Eustan Williams, Githavul tribe

Some people say that Dirrangun is a witch, that she's mean and cunning and brings you all the mischief in the world. Others say that she's friendly. But she's a very old woman and she has long hair down to her knees.

Dirrangun had two married daughters and a son-in-law. This son-in-law was a *buloogan*, a well-built, handsome man. The daughters of the Dirrangun were his two wives.

As far as I can make out from the old people, these two daughters quarrelled with their mother and the *buloogan* took the quarrel up and sided with his wives. They starved the old woman; they didn't pass her anything to have a feed.

Dirrangun's camp was under a big fig-tree, here at this waterfall which is the source of the Clarence River. There was a basin here, a hollow in the rock, which contained the water. Dooloomi was the name of the pool. It was the *jurraveel*, the home of the spirit of the water. Tooloom now is the white man's name for this waterfall. Tooloom is the nearest he could get to saying Dooloomi.

While the son-in-law and his two wives were out hunting and gathering food, Dirrangun drained the water out of the pool with a bark coolamon. Some people say that she put the fire out, too, so that there was no fire in the world.

When the *buloogan* and his two wives came home in the evening, there was no water. The two wives were running about all over the place looking for water. But there was no water. Dirrangun had put leaves and bark over the empty basin hole in the rock so that the place was hidden. For two or three days the *buloogan* and his wives could not get a drink of water.

Dirrangun was pretending to cry for them. Some people say that Dirrangun was sitting on this coolamon of water in her camp, hiding it. These people say that when the *buloogan* found this out, he got angry and cried, 'Well, you're not going

80

to have all the water! I'll let it out!' He thrust his spear into that coolamon, *biggi* we call it, and let it out.

Others say that when Dirrangun, the *buloogan* and his two wives went to sleep, the *buloogan*'s two dogs, who were thirsty, found the water which Dirrangun had hidden in the coolamon. You see those two mountains? They were called Dillalea and Kalloo-Guthun. They are named after those two dogs.

In the night those two dogs returned to the camp of the *buloogan* and stood over him. And the water dripped from their mouths. When the *buloogan* felt this he woke up. He followed the two dogs back to where Dirrangun was asleep with the hidden water.

When the *buloogan* saw where the water was hidden, he was angry. He made a big rain, a big pour-down rain. The hollow rock-basin began to fill. The water rose and rose and backed up where this creek is now.

Some say that when the water began to rise Dirrangun climbed into the fig-tree and made a platform in the boughs. But the water rose and swept her and the fig-tree away and left this hollow beneath these cliffs where the waterfall is now.

Dirrangun was holding on to the fig-tree as she was swept away. She was swept over the second fall, which we call Ngalumbeh. At the bottom of this fall she was whirled round and round, still holding on to the fig-tree, in a whirlpool for half a day.

The water was getting stronger and stronger. The *buloogan* had cursed the water to make it unmanageable. It took her and the fig-tree away down into the Clarence River. From time to time Dirrangun would sit in the torrent with her legs wide apart trying to block the water, but each time the flood would bear her away.

Where the South River comes into this river, Dirrangun sat with her legs outspread. The water rose and went up and made the South River. There she sat until the flood rose and swept her and the fig-tree on again.

Below Grafton on the river there is a fig-tree growing. Many old men would see that fig-tree and say, 'Oh, look!

Dooloomi borrgun!' This means, 'That fig-tree belongs to Tooloom!' Those old men would say, 'Dirrangun. She's away down there, but she belongs up there at Tooloom.'

And I'm told that Dirrangun is still in that fig-tree below Grafton.

Dirrangun at Baryulgil
Related by Lucy Daly, Bunjalung tribe

Somewhere in the mountains near Tooloom, in those forests of tall trees, somewhere in those mountains hidden by drifting mists, the old woman Dirrangun kept hidden her sacred spring.

This old woman didn't want anyone to know where the water was. It was good water and she used to get it herself. But one day she was sick. And there was a young man called a *bulagaan*. He was a very well-built young man, he was handsome. She asked this *bulagaan* if he would go and get the water. She sent him up to this secret spring to get the water.

She had to direct him and tell where it was. So the *bulagaan* set off into the mountains to get some of the water in a bark coolamon.

When the *bulagaan* got to the water he found that Dirrangun had dammed the water up. The *bulagaan* broke the dam and the water started to run away.

When Dirrangun saw the water coming, she started to try and dam the water. But the water broke through them.

And at last the water came down and went into the sea which we call in the language *Burraga*.

That's how this river, the Clarence, came to be here. This Mount Ogilvie here, that's one of the dams Dirrangun made.

The gorge down below Baryulgil here is the place of the last dam that Dirrangun made. But the water broke through.

When the water got down to Yamba, Dirrangun realised that she couldn't stop it, so she cursed it and made it salt so that no one could drink it.

Somewhere in the mouth of the Clarence is the last stand of Dirrangun as she tried to stop the water. She threw herself in front of the water to try and stop it with herself, but the water just rushed over her and she was turned into stone.

Dirrangun at Yamba

Related by Bella Laurie, Yeagirr tribe

A long time ago in the early days there was a tribe on this side
of the river in Yamba and a family, just a family, at Iluka,
straight across the river from here. The tribe from here was
invited to go over the river and visit this family. And this old
Dirrangun, she was a cranky old lady, she was the mother of
this family.

And when the tribe from here went over to Iluka to have a
day with his family, Dirrangun wouldn't offer them anything
to eat, she was that cranky.

And she had a daughter-in-law and one son and a daughter. Everyone that went there found that she would never offer
them anything to eat. This old woman was terrible wicked
and mean.

Her son had two little boys, and the daughter died and the
daughter-in-law died and left her there with the son and two
grandsons. That's the old Dirrangun I'm talking about.

And then, they tell us that the sea was calm then, at that
time. And the son made up his mind to go away with the two
boys and leave his mother.

So he got to work and made a canoe. When he had finished
the canoe he took it down to the beach. He put one boy at the
back of the canoe and one in front. Then he got in and started
to paddle away.

The mother followed him to the beach and she didn't want
the son to go. But he wouldn't stop, he took no notice of her.

She sang out after they got a good bit out on the water in
the canoe. She called out and told them not to leave her on
her own.

She had a yam-stick with her and, when he didn't take any
notice, she started to hit the water. And she started to corroboree, sticking the yam-stick in the ground and cursing.
She started to tell the waves and sea and the water to be
rough, the wind to come and the water to rise. And she cried
and coo-eed for them to come back, but they took no notice.

So she watched them until they got out of sight. The canoe was on its way to Ballina. And just when they turned the little canoe to go into Ballina, the waves came up and the canoe sank and went under with the two little boys and the father.

And today they say you can still go to Ballina and they can show you that canoe with the two boys, one in front and one at the back, and with the father holding on to the paddle in the middle. They were turned into rock.

Then, two or three years after, the Dirrangun jumped into the river and drowned herself. There you'll hear that roar of the sea, that noise. That's supposed to be Dirrangun looking for her son and two grandboys. You'll hear that sound at Eungarri and Shelly Beach and it works right back to Ballina. That's her under the water, and she turned into a big rock.

You might have heard of those white men blasting that stone, in the mouth of the river at Iluka. That's her. They can't touch it. They can't interfere with it. They tried, but they can't.

And the white people asked my father if it would be right if they blew that stone up. My father said, 'No. If they did, all the sea water would rush in.' She's supposed to block it.

That's the true thing that the old people told us.

My father, he used to get all us children and tell us. He said, 'Whenever you hear the roar of the sea, that's Dirrangun. She's looking for her son and two grandchildren.'

My father told the white people, 'Don't touch that rock.' The white people tried and it rained and rained and wouldn't allow any boat to go out to sea. They had to leave that stone and it's still there to this day.

The Sacred Spring
Related by Ken Gordon, Bunjalung tribe

This story is a *budgeram*. When the old people said *budgeram*, they meant, 'Away back from the beginning.' In the beginning of the world there were three people. There were Ngudjungulli, Buloogan and Gaungun.

Ngudjungulli is the boss of the whole world. He never dies. Buloogan and Gaungun, they both died. Buloogan was the most handsome man in the whole world. Gaungun was the most beautiful woman in the whole world. Buloogan died, but he's supposed to come back some day. He's above all these wee-uns, the clever-fellers.

From the beginning, this land was one whole land from here to India. The aborigines used to go over and fight the Indians and come back again. The old people said that the people they fought had a kind of turban thing slip off and you'd see their long hair all fall down backwards.

There was a sacred spring in Queensland. No one was allowed to go near it.

Once, when the aborigines wanted to go over to India to fight, there was one man who had two wives. He didn't want his wives to follow him to India. So he took his nulla-nulla and half killed them both. Then he went over and left those two women behind.

When the men were gone, these two women put their heads together. 'Now, we'll go to the sacred spring,' they said.

Well, they took their yam-sticks to that sacred spring. From the spring, one went digging this way and one went digging that way. 'We'll keep going till we meet one another,' they said. As they dug, the water from the spring followed them. Where they met, one water goes this way and the other water goes the other way. It is the roughest water in the world.

Well, these aborigines finished their war over on the other side. They started on their way back. When they got along a bit they saw just one mass of water.

This Buloogan was with them. He made the mountains and islands rise out of the water. Then, with their *borror*, the string that they pull out of their mouths, the clever-fellers took this cord and threw it from island to island. They crossed over this cord until they landed back in Australia.

As soon as they came back they knew what had happened. They blamed that man for beating up his two wives.

These warriors came across those two women talking at the Australian Bight. One of the wee-uns, the clever-fellers, turned those two women into stone.

After that the aborigines lost touch with the outside world. They never went back fighting any more. This was in the beginning of the world.

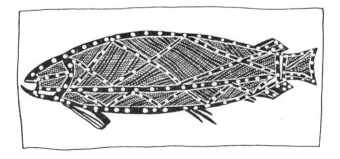

The Fairy Emus

Related by Charlotte Williams, Gindavul tribe

A big rock stands in the sea six miles out from Byron Bay. A man called Nguthungulli made that rock. Nguthungulli is our Father. He's the Father of the whole world. He's the man we've got to be afraid of. No matter what we do wrong, or where we do it, He'll know. And no man has seen Him.

Nguthungulli had a cave in the rock. After He made the rock, He told the four fairy women, *gilarmavell*, to stay there.

Then He went away from there and walked inland from the coast. He travelled over the mountains with His dog Korung. He had a walking stick, and when He put the stick into the ground He left behind a stone like a basin.

As He travelled He left the bean-trees, and He named the different places on His journeys. He named Woodenbong, where we are now, Nguthumbung.

He went over the range to the head of the Condamine. When He knelt down at the river to drink, He left His hand-prints and His knee-prints there in the stone.

Nguthungulli went away out into the desert, towards the sunset. In our language we say that Nguthungulli is away out in the *borrgorr* now, that means the sea.

The old people knew that the sea was out there. They knew that whichever way the *butheram*, the story of Nguthungulli, went, it was towards the sea. The old people had been away out west, they had seen the sea, *borrgorr*. You can hear the sound of the sea in that word. They had seen then that we were on an island.

Nguthungulli has big rocks out in the *borrgorr*, the sea, where He lives today. Out in the caves in those rocks in the sea, Nguthungulli has four daughters and one son. And His son is called Yar Birrain.

There were two brothers called Wao and Jarring. When Jarring died, Wao came over to the place called Correelya in these mountains. Wao went after those two emus which were the *barnyunbee*, the spirit of Jarring.

But the emus kept moving away. Wao kept on going after those emus day after day. When the emus had a rest, he would have a rest. When the emus would get up and go on, Wao would go on after them.

He had no time to make tea or anything. He had to keep going day after day and rest at night until he got to where Nguthungulli was in the rocks in the *borrgorr*, the sea, in the sunset.

Wao had been chasing those emus for months. He wanted them for his own *barnyunbee*, his property, his totem. When the emus came to the sea, they lay down on the beach. When Wao came up close to those emus, a fairy man called Tjoolorr came out of the sea and asked Wao, 'What are you after?'

Wao said, 'I am after them,' pointing to the emus.

Tjoolorr said, 'You can't take them. They belong to Nguthungulli.'

Tjoolorr asked Wao what he wanted to do and Wao said he wanted to stay three days, *'Borrorr yabborr.'* That means 'two and one' — three days.

And when Wao had stayed there three days, the fairy man Yar Birrain came and took Wao out to the rocks in the sea. But Wao couldn't see Yar Birrain. Yar Birrain took Wao out to the rocks in the sea where Nguthungulli is. Wao stayed three days inside that rock. And the fairy women told him, 'You can't see Nthung, Father. You can hear Him talking, but you can't see Him.' Yar Birrain told Wao, too, 'You can't see Father, though you can hear Him when He talks.'

Wao stayed there only three days and then left that place. Wao couldn't open the door by himself, not Wao, he couldn't. Yar Birrain opened the door and told him not to look back when he put his foot down on the path over the sea, but to go straight for the land.

When Wao landed back on the beach, he was back with Tjoolorr. He had to come to Tjoolorr. When Wao came to the beach where Tjoolorr was, Nguthungulli made a song about

Wao. He said 'I can't give those emus, but I will give you this song.'

Then Nguthungulli sang this song to Wao:

> Ah, Wao, why were you walking after
>   those two fairy emus?
> Wao, that was your brother's spirit,
>   those fairy emus.
> Those emus are Mine. I own them again.
> Those emus, your brother's spirit,
>   have come back to Me.

Then Wao travelled back to this country and brought the song back with him.

Wao's white name was Tommy McCauley. For a long time he was the shepherd for old Tom Hill, who owned Ngunumbar Station. And Wao died at Bungorrthun which the white man call The Risk.

The Song of Wao
Related by Charlotte Williams, Gilhavul tribe

Since in another country,
my brother, Djarring, died,
I, Wao, cross the ranges
to their western side.

Two emus there are feeding
they move away together,
two emus who inherit
the spirit of my brother.

O, that I could outpace them,
and head them back at length.
Towards the west I chase them
with all my speed and strength.

Tired, my limbs seem tethered.
The morning star has gone.
The emus, ruffling their feathers,
rise and journey on.

My country far behind me
and still, day after day,
through sands that burn and blind me,
those emus walk away.

It is the gleaming ocean,
the ocean in the west.
There, on the beach, those emus
sink down at last to rest.

There, as I walk towards them,
a man comes from the sea.
'Ah, Wao, leave those emus,'
he says, 'and come with me.'

A path out to a mountain
in the sea we find.
A cavern there receives us.
The rocks close to behind.

Inside that hollow mountain
I must remain three days.
I hear our Father singing.
I do not see His face.

'Why were you walking, Wao,
through sands and forest loam
after those spirit emus?
Your Father called them home.'

The rock is cleft asunder.
I wake. The beach appears
deserted and the thunder
of breakers fills my ears.

Walking towards the sunrise,
I, Wao, now must start,
Wao, who holds the song of
our Father in his heart.

Song, for which through deserts
my feet have worn and bend,
I bear now from the Island
of the Spirits of the Dead.

Geerdung the Maker
Related by Thomas Kelly, Gumbangirr tribe

Kelly isn't my name. It's just the nearest the white man gets
to saying it. It's like all the native names of places and towns,
they're just the nearest the white man got to saying them.

My great-grandmother was Margaret Kelly, of Bowraville. She was
a princess. Her father was 'King' Moodie. She belonged to the
oldest family on the Nambucca River. She was one of the best
known in the district. She was a princess among our people and
she belonged to the Gumbangirr tribe.

My great-grandmother had the first joint of the little finger of
her left hand taken off. She was bitten by a red-back spider on
that finger. A *ngaloongirr*, a clever-feller, doctored her. He
took off that finger joint. One evening there was a terrific
great storm, lightning, thunder and a dry wind. The wind was
almost tearing the shack apart. The crashes of thunder would
deafen you, and the lightning, chain lightning, was dancing and
striking the ground.

That old lady, the princess, went out into the storm, out into
the wind, the thunder and the lightning, and directed the little
finger of her left hand up to Heaven, to *Geerdung*, our God.

He's someone we all look up to. I couldn't explain that word to
you. *Geerdung* is a lot of words wrapped up in one. It means
everything. It means everything that is beautiful.

The old lady called on *Geerdung* to protect us. Within minutes,
there was a terrific clap of thunder. Something was hit. We
looked out of the window and a big turpentine tree, eight or
nine feet girth, had been struck by lightning. The tree was
twisting from the butt in the wind. The wind was tearing it.
You could hear the grinding of the tree as it was being torn by
the wind.

That tree was thrown over the road, a hundred yards below the hut, over the South Arm road. Then the old lady came back into the hut and just lay down and said to us, 'Everything will be all right. *Geerdung* will look after us.'

As the old lady lay there that storm began to die away, until everything was quiet. We went out and had a look at that tree. It was split and shattered from the thunderbolt. Huge splinters of wood, that a man couldn't carry, were hurled hundreds of yards away. The hut wasn't touched.

The same old lady told us, two nights before she died, that she was going home to *Geerdung* the Maker. On the last night before she died, she said to all her children and grandchildren, 'Don't wake me up in the morning because I won't be there.'

The Sermon of the Birds
Related by Alec Vesper, Gullibul tribe

I was clearing thirty or forty acres once
out on the western range near Nightcap Mountain.
And as I was working I heard a gathering of crows
singing out in a jungle gully. Their clamorous cries
drawed the attention of all the other birds,
jackass and butcher bird, soldier bird, sparrow bird,
scrub robin, magpie, the black and the white cockatoo,
they all flew down to the crows in the jungle gully.

And I followed their clamour, and in the midst
of all the splendid excitement of all the birds,
I heard one fellow was singing above them all.
It was the lyrebird, the mimic of all the scrub.
And they held this beautiful sermon for half an hour.
The birds would stop and listen awhile, but still
that beautiful voice, the lyrebird, would keep on singing
and draw them and join them all to a chorus again.

As I stood there and listened, the Scriptures was
hitting me all the time. That sermon seemed
like the prophecy when Christ shall come and summon
the birds, the valleys and the hills, the mountains and ocean
to sing in praise of the grace and the reckoning day,
and the beauty of the earth in the splendour that He created.
And I went back and told my people of what I had seen,
of the sermon of praise I heard on the mountain range.